LEARN
ABC

LEARN ABC by Shawn Azami

ISBN: 979-8555047793 © 2022

Table of Contents

Contents	Page

Table of Contents [cont.]

Contents	Page

----A--a----

ALLIGATOR

----A--a----

ANT

----B--b----

BEAR

----B--b----

BEE

----C---c----

CAT

----C---c----

CHICKEN

----D--d----

DEER

----D--d----

DOLPHIN

----E--e----

EAGLE

----E--e----

ELEPHANT

-----F--f----

FISH

-----F--f----

FROG

-----G--g---

GIRAFFE

----G--g---

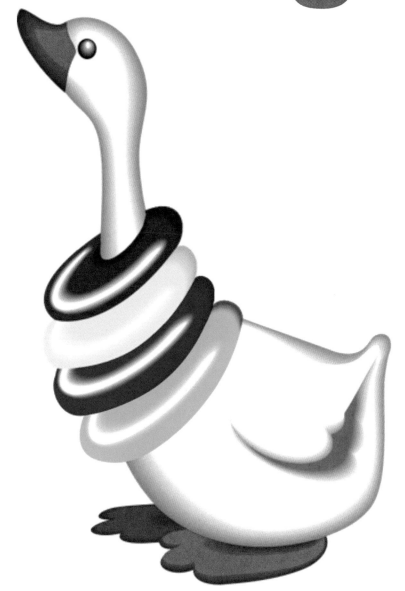

GOOSE

----H--h----

HORSE

----H--h----

HUMMINGBIRD

IGUANA

INCHWORM

-----J--j----

JAGUAR

-----J--j----

JELLYFISH

----K--k----

KANGAROO

----K--k----

KOALA

L--l

LADYBUG

LION

---M--m---

MONKEY

---M--m---

MULE

----N--n----

NIGHTINGALE

-----N--n-----

NUMBAT

OCTOPUS

OSTRICH

----P--p----

PEACOCK

----P--p----

PIG

-----Q--q---

QUAIL

----Q--q---

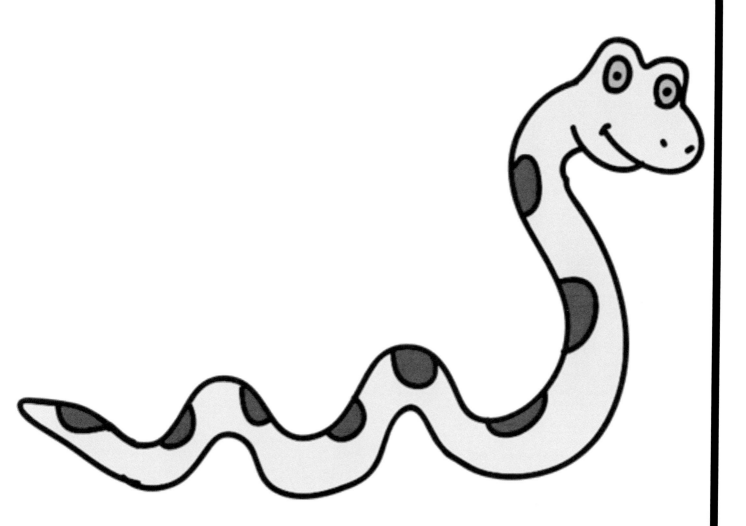

QUEEN SNAKE

----R--r----

RABBIT

----R--r----

ROOSTER

----S--s----

SEAL

----S--s----

SHEEP

------T--t----

TIGER

-----T--t----

TURTLE

----U--u----

UINTA CHIPMUNK

----U--u----

UNICORN

V v

VAMPIRE BAT

----V--v----

VULTURE

---W--w---

WALRUS

---W--w---

WHALE

----X--x----

XERCES BLUE

----X--x----

X-RAY FISH

----Y--y----

YABBY

-----Y--y-----

YAK

----Z--z----

ZEBRA

----Z---z----

ZORILLA

About the Author

Shawn Azami

Shawn grew up in Fresno, California excelling in mathematics in school, taking Calculus as a high school Junior and Calculus II as a Senior. At 18, Shawn was accepted to Cal Poly San Luis Obispo, where he earned degrees in Electrical Engineering and Mathematics, with a minor in Philosophy.

Always active in sports as a teenager and young adult, Shawn wrestled and played soccer. Currently he enjoys playing squash and racquetball and is a USTA tennis member.

Shawn's most sold work, *"MATH GAMES"*, slowly emerged as he created card games to help his friend's and family's younger children learn math and critical thinking while still having fun.

"MY ALPHABET" and **"LEARN ABC"** were suggested since the younger ones really loved the animations and graphics.

Currently living in his second residence in Fresno, California, Shawn teaches math and runs his own website:

www.FresnoMathTutoring.com

Image Acknowledgments

Image Acknowledgments

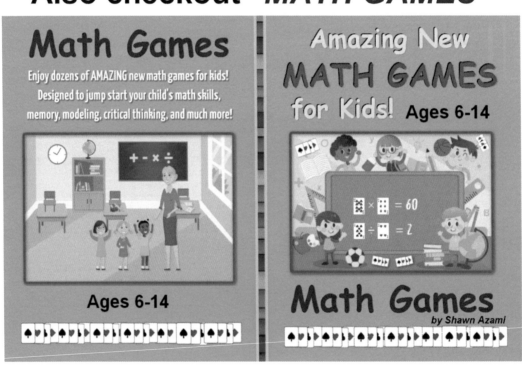

Made in USA © 2022

55

Made in the USA
Las Vegas, NV
20 November 2024

11584583R00036